LOVE

BY JOHN CASTAGNINI

Cover Concept: John Castagnini, Gio Sebastian
Cover Design: Gio Sebastian
Editing: Lea Sandham, Matt Reagan, Lorraine Garnett
Type Design: Lorraine Garnett

"Love," by John Castagnini. ISBN 978-1-951985-72-1 (softcover); 978-1-951985-80-6 (eBook).

CONTENTS

DEDICATION

Over this past decade, my brother-in-laws, Eddie Dillon and John Dillon Jr., and my cousin, Stephen Mazarra, passed on in their early 50s.

Thank you for the amazing moments that we shared.

Thank you for reminding me (as I hit my 50th) to reflect each day, to reach deeper inside, to shine even brighter, as I inevitably join you all eventually in fading away...

LOVE

BY JOHN CASTAGNINI

I: POEMS

Reach

No matter the burning buried inside,
 there remain the stars,
 the fire in the sky.
Though trees and mountains have been
a sanctuary in years past.
I climbed them both and witnessed mankind level
its path.
But the stars remain burning, twinkling,
shooting through the skies,
only wonder and possibility for Heaven's billion
eyes.
I reach for you,
dream to touch,
aware of the futility.
But what's a star to reach for,
where to find its humility?
Thank you, stars.
Without you would there be not only light,
but any reason for dreaming through the night?

TAKE IT

You've taken part of me.
I'd rather you have it.
Take this part you left behind.
It's the most precious.
It breathes my life, it's so heavy,
it sank to the bottom of my heart.
I can't get it out.
It's you. It's yours.
Take it away.
Is it fear? Is it me?
Has it become me?
Ultimately I concede.
To what's best for you.
You decide.
In between you and me,
lies eternity and whatever we imagine.
In between you and me,
is nothing.

WHERE?

Where are you?
Nestled within the crystal blue sparkling
eyes of a precious newborn?
Or hiding in the harmony of the sparrow
rejoicing in the awakening of another dawn?
Are you?
Dancing between the raindrops
enveloped amid the nimbus clouds
glittering within the rainbow's guiding light?
Or singing a symphony of stars
cradled in the moon,
tucked within the solitude of another lonesome
night?
Maybe you are?
In the pain and fear that binds us to the history of
a suffering that's forever plagued mankind...
Or...
In the gain and loss that blinds us to the mystery of
a loving we have only faith to find.
Did you find it?
Beyond the illusion,
Beside its elusion,
Within the delusion of confusion,
Within EVERY conclusion.

L❂V E

NOWHERE ELSE

Each entry is an exit.
Every exit, an entry.
On the road from nowhere,
to nowhere else,
somewhere in your mind...

LIVING

You can't drink it away,
or fuck it any harder.
Not a friend nor family,
can change its course.
Ultimately subdued by the majesty of life,
and the course of living.

BURY

Bury the way to your heart,
beneath the weight of the world.
This day I die,
the day I decide not to die anymore.

Rocks

You've taken part of me,
    I'd rather you have it.
    Please take this part you left behind...
It's the most precious.
It breathes me life.
It's so heavy,
It sank to the bottom of my heart.
I can't get it out.
It's you.
It's yours.
Take it away.
Fear?
Is it me at all?
Has it become me?
I concede to what's best for you.
You decide.
Go away, come back...
I will rest.

L☯VE

WHEN

Remembering when I didn't remember when...
is a place I've completely forgotten.

MT

Carry no umbrellas to this
empty page.
Break the big glass window
in front of you.

UNKNOWN

To sound smart,
to perceive pride,
to walk wise,
to remain remembered...
What a load of bullshit.
The generations to come
will build who you are.

I: POEMS

BETWEEN

A thousand geese to my right,
march in a straight line.
A thousand graves to my left,
lying in a straight line.
I stand still on the paved road in between them...
Half the geese cross over to the left,
I still stand between them.

IN BETWEEN

Life is therapy...
And death is the cure.

UP

The more I gaze upon the crevices,
in a single blade of grass,
the more every stem
in the field in front of me,
shows its ass.

L☯VE

Wake up and go to sleep.
You die in being born.

SeeSay

Between you and me, I stand.
A ubiquitous dance.
Deafening our eyes.
With no lead we follow.
Imagining with all our might,
something grander than perfection.
Blinding our ears,
rejoice in this insatiable quest.
Discovery content in its reward,
the 'nothing' you will ever find - and dance.

See

Hiding grey eyes behind my
Gucci glasses.

AM NONAM

I am the poet I will never be.

U

Listen closely enough,
to hear God's echo surrounding you.
Beyond the cleverness
of any thoughts impeding your remembrance,
the pure genius of you.
A brilliant mind,
an open heart.
A perfect soul,
be you.

SPACE

In between you and me,
lies eternity and whatever we imagine.
In between you and me,
is nothing.
A place where everything can be found,
in discovering one another.

L ☯ V E

WRIGHT

A poet is written...

MEASURE

The world is filled with
inadequate adequacy.

GRAVE

You're right there in front of me,
your final resting place on earth.
I love these trees guarding your
days and nights.
Like father and mother, you stand together,
in a straight line.

I: Poems

Knowun

Crying in the rain,
imagining I'm sheltered.
I'd rather be washed away.
Im drenched,
drowning in all the love around me.
To let it go,
to let it in,
to let it be.
Who are you?
I'm yours forever,
and you will never be mine,
though you and I
open the sky.

L ☯ V E

S ide by side,
I stand in your shadow,
but I still see the light.
Sheltered, I give you color.
From this place,
I can write anything
and everything in wanting,
and needing nothing.
You speak,
I simply listen.
Your days sown,
I imagine mine gone.
You speak,
I'll try to listen.

STRAIN

S train not your eyes peering,
beyond the reflection.
The invisible finger steering,
in every direction.

GIFT

W earing a ring of fluorescent rainbows.
Veiled only by the golden promises.
Wrapped tightly around a wide open hand,
and a broken heart.

WALKON

D irty streets,
filthy feet,
beautiful sunrise.
What's a sign?
Tricking my mind,
beautiful sunrise.

L ☯ V E

BORN

The bright light welcomes our being.
Smack, in the ass.
Every day we are taught 'how to be.'
Eventually the moment comes...
We make life's greatest choice.
We ignite to burn brighter OR
fade away into oblivion.
As each sorrow bears in mind,
the temptation to dim our light
becomes more convincing.
More of a beacon, to carry us closer
to the ONLY understanding of man.

SIMPLY

To simply be.
This understanding truly reveals
our helpless condition.
Beyond our illusion of help,
being needed, into the illusion of the orchestra,
our symphony leads us to be...again.

DIG

I know these words will fail,
to bring any comfort to many.
But, comfort is not what I profess.
I seek only to understand.
Perhaps this seeking is a mistake,
I just haven't found another way to bring glory,
to Life's majesty.
And although, the more I see...
and the more I understand,
the next moment carries with it
more confusion.
Thank you,
I continue to come to the conclusion - I feel, I
love, I hurt,
I cry, I rejoice, and I seek, and I seek, and I seek.
Each day, another door to watch,
you open my heart and my mind.
As I encounter all these other minds,
I only ask for them to search for thee,
dig deeper into love,
look past the fear binding you,
and the light will burn brighter.
Yes...there is ONLY brighter.

HORROR

Here comes that horror again...
Thank you.
I pray for the strength of another day,
to burn brighter,
to see more.

SHOUT

Go ahead, shout louder.
I've pleaded for eternity,
a gentle whisper,
deafened, reborn.
Through embracing the breath,
amidst the stillness.
Between each heart-beat.

SHOUT LOUDER

Shouting louder, won't help the one who seeks
your gentle whisper.

ANGELS

Will we ever be done
fantasizing about memories of angels?
Ignorant and complacent,
as they glide by our side?

MORE

Just because there will always be more,
doesn't mean that there can be an iota of more.

CREATE

It is in our denial,
where we become,
the Creator.

L ☯ V E

HERE

The more over here, is the same as the more
over there. Pretend
Seeking more over there, can imprison one
to 'the less,' where they are.
Seeking more over there, can lead one to
everything, where they are.

MY WAY

I come to this page,
when I can no longer persist.
I come to this page because - the pounding
persists.
My way is so different from the world I explore.
My heart and mind enslaved,
chained to God's door.
While the many insist in the delusion of their
freedom,
like a fool to the one,
I enlist in the conclusion.
It's her Kingdom,
and his rules.

HERE

I am here.
The expectations of others make me invisible,
I only asked to be honored where I am.
Others may sense it,
Non-attachment is the key to sharing the fullness,
of now.

PAIN

I'm asking for guidance beyond
the knowing of the perfection
in whatever way...
Doesn't stop my mind from
trying to chase away the pain.

I KNOW

At least I know
so much more than I know.

Sky

Your sky carried the burdens
away for a moment,
how grand your sky.
How small am I.

Go

Submission and loss,
both illusions,
addictions and love.
Both conclusions.
Those outside, pretend to understand.
Those beside me,
expect more than I hold in my hands, with my
heart.
It's enough,
until it's not.
I will share as I am,
who I can really be.
The one who honors this,
will stay.

ALONE

Thankful for this day,
nervous, fearful, tortured,
hopeful, wishful, amazed
and amused.
I'm stuck, I'm free,
I'm content,
I'm disgusted,
I'm alone.
With one, or two, or all,
I'm alone.
I am thankful for this day.

A MUSE

Our confusion is God's amusement

ALREADY

A true artist creates what's already there.

PROOF

The truth is a lie.
  Only deeper inside,
the proof is a lie,
that's safer to hide.

EVERY DAY

I die a life, a lie - Every day.

ASK

There's no new way,
  so it is, they say.
Yet, we all scream to be heard.
We would rather obliterate ourselves,
than be told. I am learning to ask.

EMPTY BOX

Most people buy an empty box.
They believe they know better,
convinced by whatever.
I know we don't,
not by knowing,
but by knowing what is not.

SHOW

The moment I stop trying,
is the moment, I am.
The fat lady in front of me,
the beauty by my side,
merge into meaninglessness.
I am here,
no one really cares,
and It's OK.
Thankful for the free ticket to life,
the greatest show on earth.

L O V E

The louder I scream,
the more silent I become.
I am love to everyone around me,
with a whisper the many, lend me an ear.

COSTUMES

To the way I respond,
is what I am committed,
to find a way beyond the costume I once
fitted.

WINGS

I've tried to replace it with so many things.
I'm always left with half.
No matter what it brings.
You'd think that an angel would make my heart
sing...
I thank her for the discovery.
I'm my own second wing.

PAUSE

I never noticed the purple tinge upon a pigeon's nape.
I never noticed how each bird differed.
From bill to tail, to cape.
I never noticed most of the world...
Until I paused the fricken tape.

NO GO

I finally found the place I was looking for,
when I finally realized there was no place else to go.

DO

People do what other people do.
Other people do what other people do.
Do what you do.

L☯VE

REAL

J ust because it is an illusion,
doesn't mean it isn't real.

REMEMBER

L overs kiss goodbye.
Gazing into each other's eyes.
Hoping through one another.
Through the coping, a fantasy or two.
Nothing more can be expected.
A simple embrace, never enough.
Submissive only, to what they fail to remember.

SAME

W elcome to a place where I give the meaning.
No longer faced with any comfort in dreaming.
Forever pretending, and ever ascending.
Imagining a difference.

POWER

The power of two appears,
twice that of one,
and then it appears even more.
The power of a thousand,
might make history.
The power of one,
is the grandest of mysteries.

SPACE

Somewhere in between 'I' and 'Love' is everything.
Beyond this is all,
All calling to me, to widen the space between 'I'
and 'Love'.

TRY

What I am trying to say,
is what I am trying to say.

L ☯ V E

JOYCE

Devils and Angels.
Casting one another,
through heaven and hell.
My cousin disappeared,
and I faced the life she feared.
She walked alone,
for all but the one,
who followed her to kingdom come.
Alone as her is who I am,
Alone like her,
is who I was not.
Alone with each other,
is who we really are.
In sharing our aloneness our oneness carries us
home.
Thank you, for being the last person I will forget
to tell.

OPEN

Open up, to let go.
Close, in order to open.
Let in, to let go.
Open up, in order to close.
Open up, to let in.
Let in, to close.
Close, in order to let go.
Let in, to open.
Close, in order to let in,
Let go, in order to close.
Let go, in order to open.
Let go, to let in.
Changing is confusing.
Confusion is changing.
Changing and confusion are illusions.
A perfect mess as one.
Smile, alone in the stillness.

L❂VE

Just because I can see the perfection,
doesn't mean I can see the perfection.

An empty page,
is an empty cage.
Waiting...

Everyone is buried, the majority are dead.
A dozen, dancing in the sky.
Three guide the way for the few.
Couples gasping for air,
anyone can join me...
As we resurrect our breath.

Through Me

Look through me and share all that you see.
Look through me…
Tell me that you found what I have been
looking for.
Look through me…
Realize my being,
realize my dreams,
capture my fears.
Look through me…
Tell me it will all be ok, that I am more than
enough.
Look through me…
Discover something, I can never.
The insatiable obsession for you to look through
me.
You'll find me, lost.
Wandering in my story.
Look through me…
Guide me through your heart, to my own.

L❂VE

BOX

Box me in
to a load too heavy to bear.
Box me in
to a shape I cannot escape.
Box me in
to a load you wish to carry.
Box me in
to the dream I am.
Box me in
to the dream I dream.
Box me in
to your deliverables.
Box me into your sensibilities.
Box me into invisibility.

YOU MESS

The Universe is a perfect mess.

HOLLOW EYES

Hollow eyes,
leave me alone.
The fox in this den
catches his meal every time.
Empty or full.
It matters no more,
to these hollow eyes.

SHADOW

Tripping over your shadow.
To be revered, to be brilliant.
How foolish I've been.

FIND ME

Spell check,
grammar check,
digitize my mind.
Fuck it, write it for me.
Find me, if you can.

THE ADDICTION TO NEED

The addiction is to the need,
to the craving to let the outside world
control us...
The need for certainty, found in being told what to
do, in what to think...
The fear is of standing out, in honoring our power,
in allowing oneself to shine,
In feeling comfortable within your power...
As most lack the worth, the value in themselves, to
see their light...
The test is in not letting yourself shrink...
Don't allow yourself to be convinced into anything
less than love who you are...
Allow yourself to shine as the star, you already are
inside...
You can tap that love, that light every day,
in every moment and co-create, whatever dream
you hold in your heart...
If you simply allow yourself to become comfortable
in the unknowing...
In transcending your addiction to need...
We allow ourselves the power we deserve...
To become who we already are.

BY JOHN CASTAGNINI

II: APHORISMS

MONEY

"Making your time more valuable than money - makes
you a lot more money."

"Follow the money and lose your heart - Follow your
heart and the money will find you."

"The way to becoming financially wealthy is to endlessly
give away the love within your heart, and allow yourself
to receive what you would truly love, in exchange."

"The ONLY way to truly master wealth, is prioritizing
living your heart, so wealth will find its way to you....
Prioritizing and working for money, is an empty road to
a life of mediocrity, at best."

"Money does NOT equate to freedom.
In fact, the responsibility and accountability that comes
with more money can put one into tremendous bondage.
Freedom 'IS'... Freedom is now... You are already free...
You are as free as you allow yourself to be...
As you allow yourself to listen to and follow your soul,
you discover true freedom.
With this freedom, you can then choose to 'participate'
with money on YOUR terms.
Here you become wealthy, where you are a master of
money, as opposed to money being a master of you."

"The single primary key to truly mastering money and wealth is to NOT prioritize it. It's to make it secondary to serving the genius that is liberated in following your heart each day."

"The world is full of opinions and lots of bad advice. Most of success comes from knowing whom to listen to for what and when to listen to yourself."

"Money is currency. A current moving as light.
Ultimately, as you liberate your light in service,
money unites with you in harmony,
transcending any perceptions, any emotional resistance.
Yes, ANYONE can learn how to do this.
Once you do, good luck stopping it. "
"As you grow your business, you discover how to choose your customers wisely, and then over-deliver in communicating clearly."

"Handling 'success' is equally as challenging as handling 'failure', and in many ways a lot more confusing."

RELATIONSHIPS

"The only emotionally abusive relationship that exists is with oneself."

"If you find yourself at odds with a self-righteous narcissist, look in the mirror and appreciate the self-righteous narcissist that you are repressing, projecting and denying."

"Most of our lives are spent misunderstanding ourselves and being misunderstood by others..."

"We visit one another's cages to free ourselves from our own."

"Sometimes your heart has to be broken to open."

"Don't trust your judgment. Trust your NON-judgment."

"Not truly listening to yourself and others causes most life challenges."

"Playing smart is often dumb... Playing dumb is often smart."

"What baffles me most about human behavior is how incessantly we rip other people to shreds, disowning and projecting these unloved parts of ourselves onto others, simply to create a state, to justify our self-righteousness."

"It's all light. Everyone and everything is experienced as a reflection of you."

"I am not you, but you are me.
You are not me, but I am you."

"Life is coming to appreciate giving and receiving love in our own unique way."

"We are each endless reflections of one another."

"People embrace, or are repelled, by the parts of themselves that they project onto their perception of you."

"If you approach people genuinely from your heart seeking to hear and understand, and you communicate from this place expressing clearly what you would appreciate in the exchange, more often than not, you will receive more than you ask for, in some way."

"We all love in completely unique ways, and some of us in very strange ways."

"We 'scream' to let love in and let love out of our own personal prison."

"Our greatest barrier to love is the box where we imagine love to be."

"The perception of love is the cause of disease. The experience of love is what heals it."

"The best way to evolve this planet is to appreciate our teachers and the systems we use to manage them."

"You are here to help each person experience more love for themselves through you as they choose."

"Truly loving a person kills a part of them as well as a part of yourself. Equally."

"Your entire life will be spent in a wrestling match between your mind and your heart liberating love."

"Facing a broken heart is one of the bravest things in life that you can do."

"The greatest gift that someone can give to you is their
genuine interest in taking their time to get to know you."

"Most people are much more comfortable being half a
person and projecting onto others the half of themselves
that they disown."

"If you appreciate each and every person in your life
for exactly who they are, your relationships become
extraordinary."

"The best way to feel loved is to love others for exactly
who they are, rather than for who we wish them to be."

"As you honor the uniqueness in each person, you
expand the unity between you and them."

"Bridging the illusion between self and others is
to *LOVE NOW!*"

"Our masculinity tends to repress our emotions.
Our femininity tends to get lost in them.
Our genius learns to integrate our being and transcend
our emotional limits."
"If everyone simply loved everyone else, the way they are...
What a wonderful, and boring place the world would be."

"Love is the problem... Love is the solution..."

"The uniting of two people, are two entire universes
 intertwining... Each person, now exploring the
 boundaries of two worlds, one completely new to them,
 and one barely traveled... As each travels to lands where
 neither has boldly gone before. They discover, reveal,
 hide, share, own, deny and embrace
 what appears to come and go, as they explore the infinite
 oneness in now, together... And apart."

"And as each day passes,
 I'm caught between falling into your arms and drifting
 further away...
 The thought of what you once loved, being gone forever
 is too much for anyone to bear.
 We'll pretend almost anything to imagine a forever.
 We'll concoct a way to swear it to the grave that surely
 awaits us...
 All in the hope of love."

"Be open enough to hear people's values and suggestions…
But wise enough to hear their imbalanced perceptions,
And their attempts to manipulate you, as you value
yourself."

"You'll imagine there's someone you're supposed to be as
you come to terms with who you have been, and who you
are. And hopefully, along the way,
you'll remember to listen to yourself,
and the people around you close enough,
to hear their dance echo in your heart…"

"Most people value what they think they can get from you.
A few are inspired to discover how they may be of service
and find a fair exchange."

"Perhaps the echo of silence between us will
wake up the world."

"Don't allow the value that another person expresses
toward you determine the value you have for yourself."

"Beside the empty spaces inside your heart…
Meet me there, and together, we shall shine the sun…"

"You may be the answer for someone today, if you are open to their question..."

"I live for my words to dance with love, inside your heart..."

"To reveal my struggle, my vulnerability, my genius, my being... My attempt to love, and be loved."

"Your soulmate IS you, and as soon as you own this, they appear in anyone YOU choose."

"By knowing and appreciating yourself, and others you become empowered to orchestrate magnificence."

"The judgments we hold of others, blind us to the love that dances right before our eyes."

"It's only your smile that I hope to embrace me, as I wander alone forever, into the unknown."

"A single goodbye can last an entire lifetime."

"Life's spent breaking down, and building up barriers, to love..."

"Everybody feels more like 'Somebody' when they feel loved by 'Someone' at some level."

"In order to see eye to eye with someone, you must first be willing and able to take a good look at yourself."

"In order to see eye to eye with someone, you must first be willing, to sit heart to heart."

LEADERSHIP

"You lead not by being better than others – You lead by bettering others…"

"In waking up each day and asking yourself; 'How can I be of great service to other people, in serving my very best to them?'… You will discover amazing things!"

"The greatest gift you can share is to simply hold a place of presence, where you truly listen to others…"

"You become more of you, by helping others become more of themselves."

"People being taught from an early age 'how' to think for themselves, and 'how' to appreciate the thinking of others… would most certainly evolve the human condition…ccWhen you are truly balanced, the emotional states of those around you turn into light."

"You discover the greatness within you, by finding the greatness all around you…
You discover the greatness all around you by finding the greatness within you."

"If you believe: 'Everyone should be playing by the same rules,' then you'll continue to follow the rules that a leader is making and breaking, themselves."

"By standing in, and sharing your loving presence - you change the world."

"Empowerment, embraces your power and your weaknesses - equally."

"Appreciation is shown in presence - not in promises."

"Great leaders are even greater followers."

"I no longer care to be respected, feared, admired or recognized - I wish only to appreciate."

"Building a 'Kingdom' before we die, we rot and vanish into the ether for eternity."

"I truly try to come from my heart, most of the time - I look for, and try to help each person that I meet, appreciate themselves, gain wisdom and see their genius…. At the same time, if I am being completely honest, there is some pervasive, delusional stupidity going on, that I gave up on…"

"Nothing, absolutely nothing, is more powerful or fulfilling, than tenaciously trying to lead your life from the kindness of your heart - No matter what."

"You evolve your vision, in aligning with the extremely powerful resources and people who are already around you."

"A woman's smile..... rules the world."

"The coward says nothing... The sage has nothing to say."

"One of the smartest things you can do, is to identify specifically, how each and every person is smarter than you."

"You light up the world, in sharing the words buried deepest in your heart."

"The more you own your own bullshit...the easier it becomes, to see through the bullshit of others, and advance to wiser choices."

"When you truly dedicate your life to serving others from your heart, you become more than you ever could have imagined yourself to be."

"You'll sink saving people, you'll soar in serving them…"

"Spend your days opening people's hearts and minds. The rest takes care of itself."

"Your words are the most valuable possession that you have. In using them wisely, in sharing them from your heart, you can manifest genius."

"Most of the time, people want you to tell them whatever will perpetuate the fantasies that they have constructed their lives around."

"Only when we prioritize sharing with our children how to liberate their genius ahead of developing their intelligence, will humanity take a leap toward unity."

"With wisdom, your highest priority becomes the quality of the conversations you have with yourself—and with others."

"Most of the time, most people care little about what you say or do… and a lot more about what they think you said or did."

"Leadership is born by remaining calm in the eye of the storm."

Grieving

"The pain from the passing of a loved one does not
subside, it amplifies. If you are blessed, you become
more able to focus that pain, to obliterate any space-
time separation between you and your loved one,
to become present with them once again
with grace in your heart."

"The hardest part of a loved one passing is not the
grieving...
It is in letting go of the grieving.
At some level, the grieving becomes the person.
At some level, we hold onto the grieving with all of our
might, as if letting go of the grieving would be letting go
of our loved one.
So much so that most of us grieve for a lifetime.
If we're blessed—if we allow ourselves to forge through
the torturous terrain of mind—we may find inner
peace in honoring our loved one's past, in appreciating
their transformation, and in letting go of the need for
anything more than an open hearted Thank-you."

"When Mother's Day comes up and your mom's dead...
There's a part of you that looks back with anger and
despair, wishing to return to all the yesterdays stuck in
your heart. There's another part of you that looks for
mom in today, and holds her close with tears of love for
who she has been, and who she will always be to you.
And a tiny part of you that pretends there is something
more, a fantasy you create to ease the pain of a never
again."

"When someone you love dies, a part of you does die with
them. When someone you love dies, a new part of you is
born with them... In this new birth, you heal grief and
expand as one together."

"Sometimes I awake to sunrise,
stabbing my eyes open to the loneliness of another day
without you...
Some days the sun blinds me to the sky, hiding your
heart from mine...
Some days... Sometimes..."

AWARENESS

"Tomorrow, I'm practicing to be more sensitive. So don't be an asshole to me, please."

"The life you believe going on inside your mind, is such a tiny insignificant perception of an infinite Universe - it ultimately means nothing at all... The next time you catch yourself caught in its web, remember this: Breathe and simply be..."

"The war in our mind stems from: our desire for a connection to, and liberation from everyone and everything, simultaneously..."

"Cancer and heart disease are often symptoms of buried emotions that your body is telling you to open up to, appreciate and let go of!"

"Any persecution of others, stems from the denial and projection of unresolved persecutions within oneself..."

"We spend a lifetime seeking the presence that we were born into..."

"Life is coming to terms with yourself…"

"HEAR yourself… and HEAL yourself…"

"Living what ONLY YOU can do BEST, is what YOU are here to do…"

"Everything in life is a double-edged sword."
"The truth is beyond any words… The truth lies beyond any mental constructs at all."

"You will know nothing… However, you can learn to love."

"Every problem in your mind is solved by breaking into your heart."

"Time does NOT heal wounds – Only a balanced perspective does."

"In letting go of who you think you are, you will find yourself…"

"The war in our mind stems from: Our desire for a connection to, and liberation from, everyone and everything… Simultaneously…"

"Don't apologize for being smarter than most people, and dumber than a few – Most people believe the same..."

"As you come to appreciate right where you are, you free yourself, to go anywhere..."

"The key to life is learning when to slow down, and when to speed up, in order to become still..."

"You will drive yourself crazy until you become present."

"As you commit to your personal interest, beyond all else - the rest falls into place."

"Your life's but a lie, painted in the sky."

"Believe in nothing with your whole mind, and believe in everything with your whole heart."

"You come to see your beauty, in appreciating your ugliness."

"You are a living contradiction, continuously coming to terms with yourself."

"Your fear will lead you to what to heal in your heart - if you let it."

"Come to believe in something, as you believe in nothing."

"How much love you put into whatever you've got is all that matters."

"You have infinite opportunities to choose from, RIGHT NOW."

"It's all light - It's all you - The rest is your illusion in space/time."

"Your life's a bump on the road. To everywhere and nowhere."

"Finding disorder gets you drugs. Finding order gets you love."

"You are a billion realities, coming to light."

"You will fit yourself into the world - as you fit the world into you."

"Music can heal most diseases - if you let it in."

"An old soul in a new world, playing the same song."

"You will find light within darkness - You will not find darkness within the light."

"Begin each day remembering, today may be your final breath. Be guided from this space, and your life will become a miraculous place."

"Our heart breaks open, as we widen our perspective."

"It's all light - The rest is your imagination."

"Whatever moral code you proclaim, you will, in some way, personally violate it."

"The illusion is that we can even possibly hold onto, or let go of anything at all."

"In evolving your consciousness, you lose your morality, and gain your heart."

"You see beyond your shadow by bringing it closer, and embracing it."

"If you're wondering why it's so difficult for loved ones, or anyone, to understand you, stop and think about what you had to go through, to understand yourself."

"Most of what you state, is in coming to terms with yourself."

"We are all one - We are all alone."

"Things are rarely, if ever, the way they seem to be."

"The more you find comfort in deeper questioning, the less you may succumb to the psychological need for, and illusion in, claiming to know anything at all."

"The most safe and most vulnerable place to be, is in your heart.

"The deeper the truth - The deeper the lies."

"You receive the most by giving your very best."

"We experience people more as we are, than as they are."

"Belief in yourself is wise - Believing yourself is myopic."

"As you discover - You become.
As you become - You discover.
The illusion of You."

"Greater truth is simply a lesser lie."

"To touch your heart - tune your mind into the sky."

"Time does not heal wounds - perspective does."

"As we come to appreciate our humanity, we discover our divinity.
As we come to appreciate our divinity, we evolve humanity."

"We're all running away from, and back to, ourselves."

"There exist Peace within War, and War within Peace - Equally."

"Life is continuously reigning in your mind, to open your heart, wider."

"While you will never be perfect - You are always perfect."

"Believing in nothing, doesn't mean believing in nothing."

"The brighter the light - The more darkness you shall see."

"Wisdom replaces knowing with incessant questioning,
for greater approximation."

"It's our reflection that blinds us from the light."

"Who you are, is not who you think you are. Yet, who you
think you are, becomes you."

"To bring out your very best, you're gonna have to deal
with your very worst…"

"The road to yourself is found alone, on the walk
between two sides."

"Sometimes, the hardest person to be is yourself, and the
hardest place to be, is where you are."

"When you are done with the clowns you keep paying to
help kill you, I am here, to help show you how to heal
yourself, beyond their inept ignorance - in my humility."

"You hear yourself, by listening beyond yourself."

"Your life is determined by the appreciation of yourself,
others and the Universe."

"People fight for the past or the future - In presence, there is no conflict."

"If you find yourself toppling a statue, perhaps reflect, and ask yourself: 'What have I not resolved, and embraced inside myself, in order to violate this statute?' I doubt the statue started it."

"Ultimately, everything returns to appreciation."

"The hand striking you is not the one to watch for."

"It's wiser to show your stupidity, and hide your intelligence, than to show your intelligence, and hide your stupidity."

"Getting rid of Depression. Impossible. Coming to appreciate Depression. Inevitable."

"Believing in yourself is ignorant - Being yourself is wise."

"The light becomes clear, as you see through your heart."

"When 'hungry' and 'humble' meet – Look out."

"What amazes me about human beings, is how much, how often, and the reasons why, we choose to stand in our own way - and what we are capable of achieving, when we finally step out of our way."

"The world will appeal to your fears and fantasies. How you respond with your mind and heart, will determine your destiny."

"Deeper conversations heal the mind and body better than any drug ever will."

"Much of the time, the wisest response is no response at all."

"The stiller you become, the faster you become."

"The road to less, and the road to more, meet in the road to nowhere."

"Loving and appreciating who you truly are, may seem a difficult road -- It is the only road."

"Find the balance in everything. Follow your heart, Listen to people's values, Save your money, Let your genius shine in grace, Dance naked in the rain, and Speak with the stars."

"An open heart and a balanced mind reveal you."

"You are the most significant insignificance in your Universe."

"Every point you try to make is pointing you inwards, to hear the other side...to resolve yourself, and balance your being."

"Expand your mind, open your heart, and allow the exchange, every day."

"What you are grateful for, is held in your heart, not in your hand."

"The greatest certainty is found within accepting no certainty at all."

"Our entire lives are spent listening to, questioning, infuriated with, negotiating with, and hoping to come to terms with ourselves... And God."

"Greet the world with an open heart, an open hand, and with one clenched fist - Ready."

"Your emotions are an imaginary prison, whose walls crumble in grace."

"We attempt to escape the same place where we long to return to - Now, beyond the lives we imagine..."

"All of the voices on the outside, are guiding you towards following the voice inside you."

"Gloomy skies widen my heart and remind me... I am not alone."

"Our lives are spent discovering, and learning how to be - who we already are."

"Most of us are here, resolving a deep personal war for a lifetime, that we alone, shall maybe see."

"In overcoming your judgments, you gain deeper and deeper access into your heart. In turn, appreciating more and more of yourself, and your life."

"It is your conversations that change your world."

"Our entire lives are spent becoming more and more comfortable, as we look deeper and deeper into the mirror, at more and more parts of ourselves."

"Thank the stress of life, for opening your heart to the divine."

"Everything in life that you are chasing, is equally chasing you. When you slow down enough to see this, it will catch up to you."

"Bipolar and "Manic Depression" are manifested delusions, created by a person, in order to escape the inevitability of rotting and dying in a Universe, that has quadrillions of imagined meanings, and no meaning at all."

"You will spend your entire life coming to terms with, and transcending all the lies that you are telling yourself."

"If you haven't figured out that you are spending your entire life bullshitting yourself, then you're REALLY bullshitting yourself."

"The ugliest places in your mind can lead you to the most beautiful spaces in your heart."

"You're really nothing more or less than manifested light... You're a million incomplete stories....with no real meaning."

"Truly having something to say... Saying it brilliantly, at the right time in space, liberates your voice and fulfills your destiny."

"Open-hearted grace - is the greatest secret to healing the mind and the body."

"Your life is a senseless riddle you imagine to solve."

"Your destiny is determined by your ability to focus, and master stilling your mind."

"In your pursuit to solve the world's problems... You may discover that not a single problem actually exists.... And that all there is for you to do, is appreciate another part of the Universe, another reflection of yourself."

"It is in elevating your conversation, through your heart, where you transcend patterns, overcome limitations and reveal the beauty of you."

"When you have something to say, say nothing at all, you will not be heard...
When you have nothing to say... Let yourself speak, and the people may hear you."

"As you own, and appreciate each of your positions in life as a unique gift, then you become able to transcend the illusion of any outward authorities, as determining who you are, what you are here to do, and who you are to ultimately become."

"Our greatest struggle in life, is in letting go of the struggle towards anything at all."

"In the space in-between pushing yourself to the end of your limit, and completely letting go of any control, and all expectation, is where you will liberate your deepest genius."

"We each are living infinite lives, in infinite moments, infinitely progressing to the fixed speed light."

"You are the greatest poem that can never be written... and is already written."

"Everything and nothing, comes from everywhere and nowhere, perfectly... Including you."

"As you come to appreciate each person, and experience of your life as a unique, equal and inseparable part of yourself... you expand the expression of your unique genius. Contributing to the eternal, musical dance of Universal presence, in love."

"You're an infinity of lies, shedding an infinite Universe to light."

"As you expand your perspective, you transcend your opinions, and discover your preferences."

"Your entire life will be spent trying to find yourself, in order to be the greater self you already are."

"With wisdom you hold no opinion on any path, only a way that you choose for yourself, that will eventually wither away."

"If you clearly see where you are a narcissist, you are probably not one.... If you cannot clearly see where you are a narcissist, you probably are one."

"Your greatest addiction is to yourself."

"Trust your intuition as you transcend your subconscious to liberate your genius."

"Open-hearted appreciation for yourself, others, and your life exactly as it is heals EVERY disease."

"Most of our lives are spent seeing what we want to see, and hearing what we want to hear. Blind to what's right in front of us, and deaf to what's actually being said."

"If you're having a difficult time letting go of something, you have the illusion that it's already gone, and you're adjusting to the transformation."

"There is nothing to believe in.
There is nothing, not to believe in.
In THAT moment, you are truly free."

"To awaken your heart, to balance your mind, to face and to transcend your addictions and fears, one by one - in order to liberate your genius... This is your destiny!"

"Manifestation from the point of infatuation, co-creates resentment in a karmic cycle... Manifestation from the state of appreciation, evolves your genius."

"If you've had moments where you've thought you're going crazy, you're probably mainly sane. If you haven't had any moments where you thought you were going crazy, you may be a bit crazy, or you're just not looking hard enough."

"War and Peace are here to stay. Each a co-creation of the other, each necessitating the existence of the other, each existing equally inside of you, as equally in the world. "

"Ultimately, your entire struggle in life will be between what you perceive, what you imagine should be, or should not be, and what is."

"Your greatest war in life will be fought between following, or not following your heart, fooling you into believing that you ever had a choice."

"It is people who take sides and positions... The truth is infinite, unknowable, undefinable - having no sides, or position at all."

"People's greatest challenge is continuously wanting to be elsewhere, and not ever finding where elsewhere is."

"Youth may be wasted on the young, wisdom is wasted on the old."

"Your body is a feedback mechanism, guiding you towards the imbalanced perceptions of your mind, as you process information in the evolution of your consciousness."

"Your life is a series of approximations, toward ever-changing illusions, rooted in nothing at all."

"It is in owning, and appreciating your own darkness, where your light begins to shine."

"No matter what you do, your entire life will be built upon the lies you are reconciling in your mind.

"The more you listen, the more you realize that almost everything being said to you, is not what's really being said."

"Overcome your ghosts and demons… and God will do the rest."

"If you're lucky, life will burn you up, and rip your heart apart."

"To drown out the noise…. Draw in the light of the stars… Let your heart open… Let your soul shine…"

"Any embarrassment we experience is our own projected, unresolved guilt, being reflected back at us, through our judgment of ourselves, and others."

"You will be a million different stories, to a million different people, none of the stories will be the same, and none of them will be true."

"At the cemetery, if you listen closely enough, you really can hear the stories of the deceased, whispering from beyond the grave."

"Our ignorance of our ignorance, is our greatest ignorance."

"You are here to unlock your own Universe, with a unique key made for you, that only you can find."

"Everything in this Universe, is nothing more than a flurry of ideas... Including you."

"You are not here to believe, and take. OR give anything...
You are here to discover how to explore, express and
exchange everything, from your heart."

"To transcend the illusive control of fear or guilt. To
follow an open hearted, present exchange from heart to
heart... This shall be your path..."

"The day that you figure out, that your entire life is
built upon a mental construct, accommodating for the
illusion of some deep-seated deficiency, you stop taking
yourself, others, and the world so seriously..."

"Always appreciative... Never satisfied."

"Everyone's simply trying to fit who they understand
themselves to be, into a world, they are trying their best
to understand. Bearing the least amount of pain, to gain
what they think will be their greatest reward..."

"Divine order and disorder are constructs within the
limited human mind...
Equal in validity, and in value..."

"Before we can realistically find a way to stop killing each other,
it might help to first learn how to stop killing ourselves..."

"No matter what it takes, no matter what hell you have to go through to do it, prioritize. Finding and living your hearts' mission, vision and purpose, as you appreciate each exchange life sends your way."

"Your life will alternate from a state of balanced, open-hearted presence, to a state of imbalanced emotional experiences, to a state of balanced, Open-hearted presence... Over and over.... and YOU determine the speed."

"We are only challenged in the moments where we fail to see the overall, omnipresent, harmonious balance in our Universe...
"As we transcend the illusion of our own personal judgments, and attachments, we align with the amazing grace, liberating our light."

"Every single thing in your life, every single word, every single experience, every single moment - is pointing you towards delving deeper into your heart...."

"Your life is the lie that you convinced yourself into... And with wisdom, you will eventually convince yourself out of it."

"Life is spent evolving the communication between your mind and your heart..."

"Life is a struggle between holding on, letting go, and letting it be..."

"Our lives are spent running away from the destiny that runs towards us..."

"At some point, we all endure the torture that we came
here to heal...
Some of us seem to get dealt a better hand, perhaps...
Ultimately, as we let go of our preconceptions, we
transcend pointing and blaming...
As the 'hoping' and 'wishing,' evolve into the light, it
leads us home... Back into our hearts..."

"All the voices on the outside, are the equal and opposite
illusions, pointing you inward, toward your authentic
being. Discovered, in the silence of presence..."

"Everything the Universe brings to you, is a gift waiting
to be opened..."

"Sometimes the people you give the most to, appreciate
you the least, and the people whom you give the least to,
appreciate you the most."

"Comparing your skills to others, can be a wise way to
improve,
Comparing yourself to others, is a waste of time."

"The wisest opinion is none at all."

"Life is a consistent unfolding of what isn't... In approaching what is."

"The life that we believe we are living, is a lie we tell ourselves in the attempt to discover our truth."

"I guess a part of me will be eternally furious at the Universe for 'taking' from me, the people whom I love the most. I guess a part of me, will be eternally grateful to the Universe for 'giving' to me, the people whom I love the most, in an infinite amount of forms..."

"Most people hide their dreams beneath a million fantasies."

"As you escape the mental constructs that imprison the mind, of what something IS, or who a person is, you become open to see, that everything and everyone, in your Universe is malleable... Here, in service with you."

"The only challenge that we each face, is a lack of understanding, interpretation and effective communication, of what is going on inside our own head."

"It is the deepest conversation inside of you, that determines your entire life."

"No matter what you say, or don't say, do, or don't do.... You will mainly be misunderstood, with most people believing that they understood you."

"Your life is already in perfect balance... No matter what you are, or are not experiencing. In honoring this perfect balance, you become free from the illusion of any chaos or disorder, and inspired or empowered, to liberate your greater light."

"Any belief co-creates a disbelief...
Any disbelief co-creates a belief...
With wisdom, we come to honor the illusion of both.
The expression of belief, holds within it, the repression of a disbelief...
And vice versa...
In 'moments' of grace, transcendent to any mental constructs - we ARE."

"Live forever in the question... Realizing, each answer as a fantasy, in a fleeting moment of infinite tomorrows."

"The most significant invention of humanity is Heaven."

"The evolution of your consciousness, your being to presence, is in transcending each judgment / position in your mind, in order to successively surrender to your heart."

"If you are going to REALLY do anything in the world, realizing, owning and appreciating, that a fair amount of people will 'THINK' that you're an asshole, is liberating and wise."

"Our lives are fantasies, compensating for the nightmares we imagine, which we are here to experience and eventually transcend..."

"The person who conquers the road to their heart, conquers their road in the world... And lives their dream."

"Our lives are spent running away from ghosts, to pursue fantasies."

"If you can't stand yourself half the time...you're not looking hard enough."

"Your life story may seem a mess... Your life is eternally perfect."

"You really are, and are not, everything that you think you are... And are NOT."

"Our greatest challenge is, the need to believe in ourselves, someone else, in something or in anything... In transcending this need, we become ourselves, present with whatever is, in the now."

"The 'today,' which may shatter your 'yesterdays'...opens you to a thousand tomorrows."

"Respect may get you the world. Appreciation gets you, your heart."

"By shifting your focus from being right, to increasing accuracy, you can expand infinitely."

"Your conversations determine your life... The management of your emotions, determines your destiny."

"The only disease....is not following your heart."

"The entire Universe rearranges itself, at least in some small way...to you."

"The key to success is learning who to listen to, for what... And above all, learning when to listen to yourself."

"Your heart is your gift to the world... Keeping it open, as you experience the world through your mind, is life's test."

"With wisdom, our Universe becomes more of something that is created through us, rather than something that happens to us."

"Most people would rather hold on to their fears than have the love and worth they fantasize about."

"Being angry over what was done, or not done, does not manifest love, it simply re-manifests more anger."

"Everyone and everything around you is a contradiction... including yourself."

"Life is a fight with yourself, in learning to love everything."

"Whether together in your aloneness, or alone in your togetherness…'tis all the same."

"Opening your mind, opens your heart. As opening your heart, opens your mind."

"It is the commitment to your heart, that opens the doors of the Universe…"

"Whatever it takes to get back into your heart…is the answer."

"You're not attracting anyone, or attracting anything… YOU ARE already everything."

"Be yourself… Knowing that anything that you think, say, or do is half the story."

"Behind every human story, is light…"

"Follow the rules, and learn when it's time to break them, and make your own…"

"With wisdom, you come to accept that God can act like a real bastard, sometimes…"

"Faith is not so much a belief in something, or anything.
It is a belief in MORE than what appears to be."

 "Whenever the Universe gives you an opportunity to
reveal your heart,
do everything you can, to take it…"

"You being who you would truly LOVE to be…
Is life's greatest challenge, and life's greatest reward."

"Any part of our life that we don't take responsibility for
in co-creating remains an unconscious illusion, that
runs our lives until we do."

"Racism is a mask that only a fool would claim, or hide
behind.
What 'exists' is the same old story of the oppressor and
oppressed.
Disguised, in a myriad of forms and colors,
all co-created between the same culprits.
Ego, Dominance and Submissiveness to Fear…"

"Every hurdle you ever face, is an illusion you created,
that persuades you from the divine, omnipresence of
now."

"Ultimately, what we all seek is appreciation in the
present moment...
With a smidgen of worship."

"You're probably a lot more beautiful, than you allow
yourself to see..."

"Finding, and living what's in your heart, is ultimately
your only option."

"Your heart bridges the life in your mind, and the life
you are living as You pay the toll."

"Every single thing that you have ever believed in life,
is a lie that you accepted, in order to coexist and adapt."

"Living the idea that you are here to surrender your life
too, is why you are here."

"Your beliefs construct, define and imprison you into a
temporary illusion of life,
for you to transcend one day... Replace, and transcend
again... Ad infinitum."

"Things don't 'turn around.' Things simply are. You 'turn around,' in order to pacify yourself, with a different illusion."

"It is the words of your heart, that lift the wings of your soul."

"It is the story that you allow, to open and close your heart... That determines your destiny."

"The last person you want to believe, and the only person to ever believe,
is, yourself..."

"Our opinions become our prisons, our refuge...
Discovered in endless questioning."

"Your life is running away from an illusion, toward another illusion...
With only a Yin-Yang to light the way."

"All the fighting in the world, with one-self, another person, between races, countries, genders and religion, ultimately stem from a fear, inciting the need to control."

"A single word, a single look or a single idea, can bring to you an entirely new world..."

"It is you, who must allow, and become comfortable with your power...
In order to allow yourself to manifest your magnificence."

"It's all a ride, on the crest of the infinite wave of your mind..."

"In becoming comfortable with contemplating, wondering, and feeling what is going on inside of you, transcending the need to know and pretend - You open the Universe to you, and yourself to it."

"Every struggle in your life, will be between letting go, and holding on..."

"Millions of dreams lie hidden behind a billion screams. Hoping to shatter their 'shackles'..."

"It is as ignorant to be an atheist as it is, to be a believer."

"The greatest challenge to the evolution of humanity, is people's overwhelming inability to discern between their opinions, and pure reason."

"Life's greatest gift is totally free. It can be accessed by anyone. It's right in front of your face,
right under your breath...
It's now... It's been there all along...
It asks for nothing..."

"You're a lot smarter than you imagine, and a whole lot dumber than you believe..."

"Your life is your pursuit of filling voids, which never existed..."

"You're better off pretending in heaven than believing in nothing if you refuse to honor eternal transformation."

"Anything other than awe and appreciation for the infinite, eternal, divine omnipresence is the delusion of your existence."

"The drive to experience complete bliss in a single object or idea supersedes all human motivation except discovering the divine revelation that hides behind transcending this bliss."

"With wisdom, you discover that there is no meaning to anything at all except the meaning you invent in order to drive yourself to expand your awareness."

"With wisdom, instead of trying to fit love into our box, we try to expand our box into love."

"The key to the spirit is to believe in nothing...in pursuing the key to you."

"What you don't love about yourself haunts your mind and engulfs your spirit until you can love it."

"There's not a single problem that cannot be transcended by clearly discovering what you would love to give, and then giving it and appreciating whatever you get in return."

'We all aspire… Yet, it appears that so few attain the significance they seek.

Perhaps the answers we seek lie in transcending our personal sagas.

Perhaps our brightest light is right beside us while we remain blind to it.

Perhaps all that you imagine is possible if you break down the walls and boxes that you fit yourself into to feel comfortable, to be safe, to feel right, to be alone.

Perhaps, if you find the gift you have to share and simply keep giving it no matter what.

Perhaps then, you will receive more than you ever dreamed…perhaps today is the way."

"Let giving love from inside your heart lead your life. Have faith that you will wisely manage whatever you receive in return."

"We yearn, we pray, we bleed, we plead for our radiance
to be what people see in us.
Because we have hidden it so well from ourselves out of
fear of it shining too bright."

"There's no one coming to save you.
In fact, there's nothing to save you from except yourself.
You'll imagine your demons into your life,
you'll wish them away, again and again,
until you can shake their hands and bid them a fond
farewell. You'll imagine you've got someplace to go,
someplace to be. And when you finally get there,
you'll realize that you have been there all along.

"Sometimes when you think you've won, you'll find you
actually lost.
Sometimes, when you think you've lost, you'll find you
actually won."

"In the end, all that will matter is: 'Are you at peace with
it in your own heart?'"

"Aligning your heart and your head is the lifelong
journey to liberating your spirit."

"With wisdom, one becomes more confident and certain,
while simultaneously questioning and doubtful."

"Society's most pervasive disease and cause of illness,
is people chasing outward fantasies instead of wisely
appreciating their being and others."

"The most disturbed person in the room is the person
who truly believes THEY are the least disturbed."

"In turning a blind eye to the broken hearts around us,
we bury our own."

"You are the manifestation of a Universal conversation
from a revolving and evolving idea."

"We each are a unique conversation of
misunderstanding and misinterpretation
on our way toward open-hearted appreciation
delivered in unification."

"There are no mistakes…
There is no success…
All is an illusion of judgment…
Everything, simply, is a momentary pattern of
perception in alternating frequencies."

"As you become OK with being alone, you come to realize
you never were, and never can be…"

"Embracing how ridiculously stupid I am…
Whilst embracing the tremendous genius I am blessed
with has been one of my life's greatest lessons."

"Our lives are spent running away from the places we
eventually long to return to and heal…"

"Blow the doors to your heart off their hinges— with
wisdom, we question. In ignorance, we react."

"We have the opportunity of resurrection in each and
every moment. Each with the same destiny. Now."

"Not knowing is as much a gift as knowing. "

"Our entire life is directed by the search for what we
perceive is missing inside us."

"Trying not to be an addict is as much an addiction as any other. And a necessary part of our growth."

"Only you can hear your heart. And only you can decide to follow it."

"The more you chase your past, the more it will elude you. The harder you try to run from your past, the more it will steal today from you."

"Nothing hurts more than the perception of uncommunicated love."

"You will spend the rest of your life learning to love yourself because everyone and everything is you.
You will spend the rest of your life discovering yourself because you reveal more of the unique you as you love each of your infinite faces."

"With wisdom, you discover:
-Nothing is as important as you think it is.
-Everything is as important as you think it is."

"The most torturous terrain you will ever endure is in climbing the mountains of your mind."

"To open people's minds, to embrace their value, their worth, and share themselves with one another."

"Beauty is a lie. It's allure, a truth that becomes more evasive the more you seek."

"While your life may sometimes seem a mess, your life story is forever perfect."

"Your own opinions are the greatest challenge to your conscious evolution."

"The most valuable friendship you will ever make is with your fears."

"Your life is imprisoned and liberated by a repeating and simultaneous ever expanding conversation."

"Learning how to appreciate the results from the difficult choices you make will heal and propel you."

"Most of us are so blinded to our own genius that we convince ourselves out of it to the point where we can't even remember what it is."

"As we drop each facade, we fall further into our heart, and deeper into the hands of God."

"Your mind guides you through your heart's terrain... The mind can be trained... While the heart can only be shut down or followed."

"There is no fairness to life.... Only the experience of creation and destruction, within the odds."

"We are all pictures, breaking through frame, after frame."

"Most of the time, people's lives are spent trying to remedy what was... Preparing for what will be... Oblivious to now."

"At a certain point, you embrace that you are completely alone, as you dance with all the illusions around you."

"The filters... Your perceptions, the judgments through which you view the world are your greatest addiction."

"We're each a prisoner to the heart...a captive to her beat."

"You are the gift of now.... As you transcend the stories of healing yesterday."

"One of the greatest ways to heal yourself is in serving others to heal themselves."

"Nothing is any better...Nothing is any worse, than this moment."

"All the voices outside of you are a reflection of all the voices inside you... Balancing one another out perfectly."

"Change itself, is an illusion of the mind... It's all now, we are simply allowing ourselves to unravel another part of what has eternally existed, all along."

"Most of our lives will be spent misunderstanding ourselves and others, in the pursuit of a fantasy."

"The lies we buy, preserve a fantasy that we wish to hold onto."

"Open your heart to the Universe, and see what happens."

"People are trying to love, just about everything, other than what's right in front of them."

L ☯ V E

"As life brings to you greater challenges, respond by opening your heart wider..."

"You are here to do something that no one else can possibly do, but you."

"The magic remains in the mind and the heart... The rest will come and go..."

"Whatever you construct, will be accompanied by equal destruction for you to wisely manage."

"Life is the free-fall into the 'nothingness' we do, and don't believe in."

"As you reveal yourself to the Universe, the Universe reveals herself to you."

"Every fight you have....is ultimately with yourself."

"The reason why so much mediocrity exists
is because people were taught that they were supposed to
be and think a certain way...
Instead of being taught how to honor, treasure and
evolve, their own unique way...
As a result, many people become uninteresting;
They fail at being programmed.
As a result, they are treated as failures,
and they actually began to believe what other people tell
them about themselves..
Their unique genius is buried, unknown to them and
the world...
It may be hard to see right now, but your genius is still
there, and you can find it...
It's why you are here...and when you get the courage to
liberate it...Your whole world evolves..."

"It's hard to believe that any person can be so ignorant
as to believe that THEY know GOD, and claim that
someone with another view, does NOT..."

"The internet is the closest thing to God that man has
created... It's revolutionizing professions, countries,
generations, our complete foundation of being... It
makes the pyramids look like a pile of rubbish..."

"In pursuing your dreams, be prepared to shatter your life..."

"As you embrace the inevitability of death,
  as you transcend the fear of losing or gaining anything,
  as you let go of the illusion that you can control anything at all....
  You become alive, open to truly living.
  A rare gift, an earth angel..."

"Your heart will break open and break into pieces as life goes on..."

"In realization, you manifest. In actualization, you transcend..."

"The only thing universal is the Universe..."

"It takes skills, NOT wisdom, to become successful...
  It takes wisdom, NOT skills, to become fulfilled....
  In aligning skills with wisdom, you become empowered to pursue mastery."

"False hope, is better than no hope at all... Most of the time."

"Each cross that you carry bends you to breakthrough."

"Follow the rules, and learn when it's time to break them, and make your own…"

"Spend your days on opening people's hearts and minds, the rest takes care of itself."

"Death can show you how to live… Hopefully, your life will show you how to die…"

"10% Reflection, 20% Imagination, 70% Appreciation"

"Sometimes our deepest love is discovered behind our greatest 'never'…"

"The best way to avoid regrets is to spend every possible moment being present…"

"Half stories run the world. Full stories run the heart…"

"You're already a star, shining bright, burning up and fading away…"

"Since everyone is fckin crazy… No-one is fckin crazy…"

"Revolving in the illusion of a denied, repressed, self-righteous persona, simply repeats bipolar patterns in your life..."

"This comedy show cannot be my life..."

"Whatever you stand up for - stands in front of you... Whatever you can't stand - stands on top of you."

"Animals and nature are the greatest healers - simply bringing you to presence."

"We have the most advanced communication systems in the world, with perhaps the worst communication in history."

"Our greatest challenge is trying to control our destiny and in surrendering at the same time."

"The key to mastery is slowing things down as much as possible, enabling you to move as fast as possible."

"I can be a selfish prick. I also have a heart of gold."

"Say: 'Fuck you' to the world, and the world will say: 'Fuck you' back. Say: 'I love you' to the world, and the world will say: 'I love you' back..."

"Words can hide your heart…Words can set you free."

"Tomorrow I'm practicing being more sensitive - so don't be an asshole towards me, please."

"The only emotionally abusive relationship that exists is with oneself."

"I Thank God for any privilege that I have, and for the challenges that come with any of those privileges."

"I think I can be an ancient astronaut theorist."

"Tyranny is sold as benevolence."

"Try to be the smartest person in the room, and be inspired when you are not."

"A woman's cry moves mountains. A woman's smile can open the skies…"

"Whatever you grab onto grips you twice as hard."

"As you look back, remember to look forward and be. As you look forward, remember to look back and be."

"Fearing and Censoring people into votes reveals desperation, not power - and it ultimately fails."

"You enlighten, as you allow yourself to transcend your beliefs, rooted in emotional attachments."

"It's OK to be afraid... We all have fears..."

"It's also OK to let go, overcome your fear, and tell the mother fckers trying to control and fear you to Fck off."

"We can heal most diseases by helping people to understand themselves better, and open their hearts."

"You overcome your addictions, as you transcend your convictions."

"I feel like we've all been sent to our rooms indefinitely by retarded parents."

"Everyone is the way they are for their own reasons."

"Your heart will break open or break into pieces as life goes on."

"Life's spent breaking down and building up barriers to love."

"In realization, you manifest. In actualization, you transcend..."

"As the genius already present in your mind meets with the love already present in your heart... Miracles open to you."

"Getting out of your own way as you step into yourself is the journey."

"You've convinced yourself into every part of your life ...
You'll convince yourself
out of your life completely
... eventually."

"Letting go of what you perceive you have, has you have it."

"Be yourself. Know that anything you think, say, or do, is half the story."

"Follow the rules. And then learn when it's time to break them and make your own."

AFTER THOUGHT

"In each passing year, we reflect on the big
changes...
Massive success...
A broken heart...
We find the love of our life...
We lose our deepest love...
And in between we breathe
preparing and praying...

The ultimate picture of life is not a pretty one...
We grow old...
Our body decays...
Sometimes the pain of life seems unbearable...

One by one, our dreams...
The people we love...
All seem to disappear.

We grab on tighter! And tighter! We tighten our hearts...
We forget to breathe...

The human condition is the one constant we all
eventually face (avoiding and pretending a bit
differently each day)...
We can build towers from here to the sky for
eternity...

But we will find ourselves in the same place—*at the mercy of what is!*

We can come to see that it's all a story...
Quintillions of stories for billions of minds...
We can discover a little more grace each day.

In surrendering to grace, we can come to terms with ourselves, each other, and the Universe, with each breath, as each story fades away...

I hope to remember and share this story of grace— the wisdom discovered beyond my illusions, beyond my emotions, hiding within a balanced mind as best I can in whatever I do each day."